13 95
R
DOV

"Brigg Fair"

and Other Favorite Orchestral Works

in Full Score

Frederick Delius

DOVER PUBLICATIONS, INC.
Mineola, New York

Bibliographical Note

This Dover edition, first published in 1997, is a new compilation of works originally published separately. F. E. C. Leuckart, Leipzig, originally published *Brigg Fair: An English Rhapsody* (1910), *A Dance Rhapsody* [*Dance Rhapsody No. 1*] (1910), and *In a Summer Garden* (1911). Universal Edition, Vienna, originally published *A Song of the High Hills*, n.d. *Two Pieces for Small Orchestra*—"On Hearing the First Cuckoo in Spring" and "Summer Night on the River"—was originally published in an authoritative edition, n.d. [1913–1914].

The Dover edition adds lists of contents and instrumentation and new headings throughout. The English text of the folk song "Brigg Fair" appeared in the Leuckart edition with a German translation by Delius' wife, Jelka Rosen. The excerpt from Eric Fenby's book on Delius, p. vii, is newly added for this edition.

International Standard Book Number: 0-486-29851-5

Manufactured in the United States of America
Dover Publications, Inc., 31 East 2nd Street, Mineola, N.Y. 11501

CONTENTS

"Brigg Fair"
and Other Favorite Orchestral Works

After supper Mrs. Delius reminded us that in a few minutes' time Sir Thomas Beecham would be broadcasting *Brigg Fair* . . . When the music had ceased, Delius called out, "Splendid, Thomas! That is how I want my music to be played. Beecham is the only conductor who has got the hang of it! That was a beautiful performance . . . Now let's clear the air and play that record of the Revellers—'Old Man River.'"

This and other such records gave him great pleasure, for the singing was reminiscent of the way his negroes used to sing out in Florida, when as a young orange-planter he had often sat up far into the night, smoking cigar after cigar, and listening to their subtle improvisations in harmony. "They showed a truly wonderful sense of musicianship and harmonic resource in the instinctive way in which they treated a melody," he added, "and, hearing their singing in such romantic surroundings, it was then and there that I first felt the urge to express myself in music."

From Eric Fenby, *Delius as I knew him*, Dover, 1994 (0-486-28042-X)

For Percy Grainger

Brigg Fair
An English Rhapsody
(1907)

BRIGG FAIR

English Folk Song

It was on the fift' of august
The weather fine and fair
Unto Brigg Fair I did repair
For Love I was inclined.

I rose up with the lark in the morning
With my heart so full of glee,
Of thinking there to meet my dear
Long time I wished to see.

I looked over my left shoulder
To see whom I could see,
And there I spied my own true love
Come tripping down to me.

I took hold of her lily white hand
And merrily was her heart,
And now we're met together
I hope we ne'er shall part.

For it's meeting is a pleasure
And parting is a grief,
But an unconstant lover
Is worse than a thief.

The green leaves they shall wither
And the branches they shall die
If ever I prove false to her,
To the girl that loves me.

INSTRUMENTATION

3 Flutes [Fl.]
2 Oboes [Ob.]
English Horn [Eng. H.]
3 Clarinets in B♭ [Cl.]
Bass Clarinet in B♭ [B.-Cl.]
3 Bassoons [B^{ns}]
Double Bassoon [D-B^{n}]

6 Horns in F
3 Trumpets in C [Trump^{s}]
3 Tenor Trombones [Tromb^{s}]
Bass Tuba [B.-Tuba]

Timpani [K(ettle) Drums]

Percussion
    Bass Drum [Big Drum]
    3 Tubular Bells [Bells (in B♭, C, D)]
    Triangle [Triang.]

Harp (*or several*)

Violins I, II [V$^{ns.}$]
Violas
Violoncellos [Cellos]
Basses

Brigg Fair
An English Rhapsody

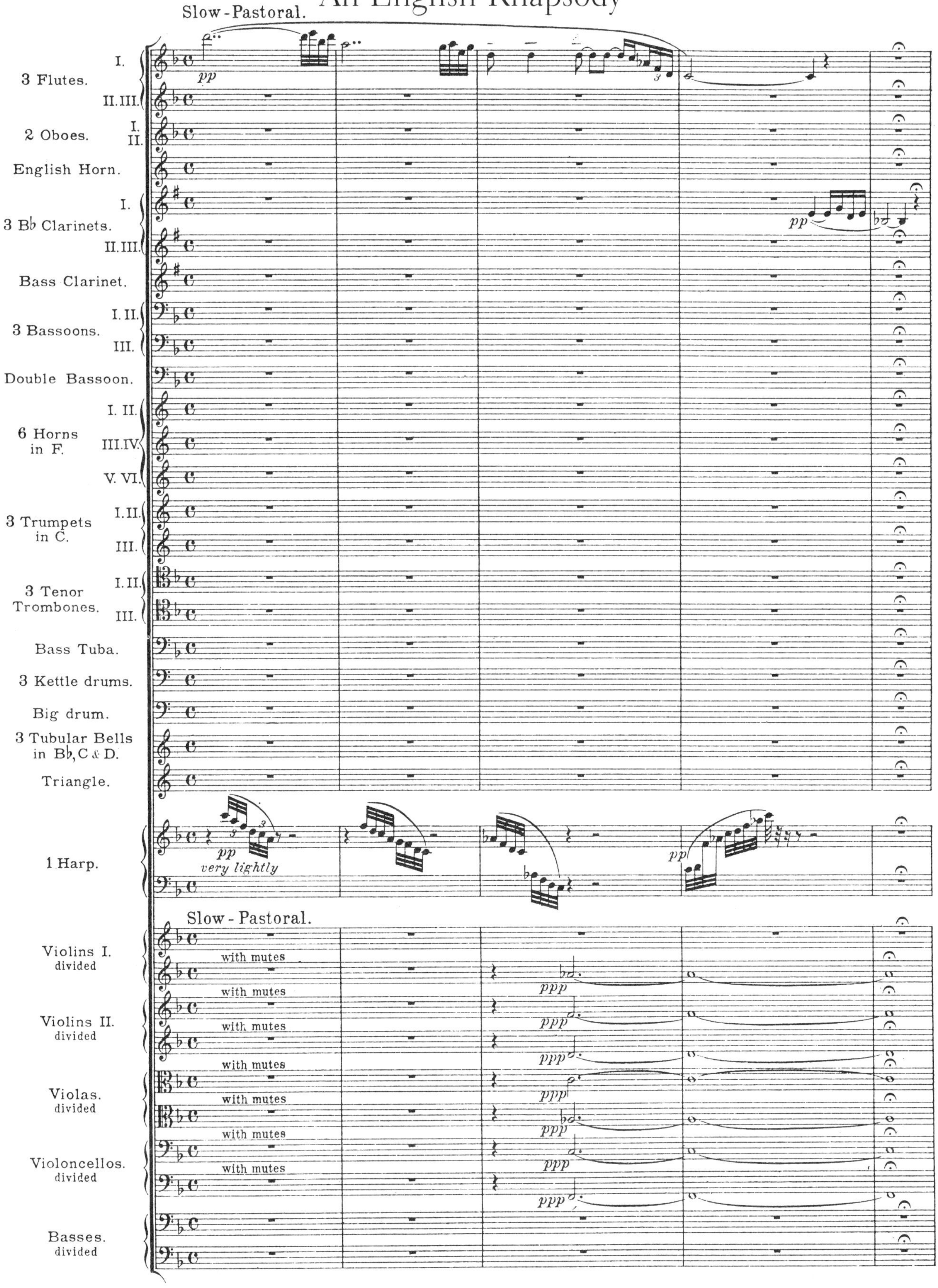

30   Brigg Fair

Brigg Fair   35

A Dance Rhapsody

[Dance Rhapsody No. 1]

(1908)

INSTRUMENTATION

3 Flutes [Flauti, Fl.]
  Fl. 3 doubles Piccolo [Picc.]
Oboe [Oboe, Ob.]
English Horn [Corno inglese, Cor. ingl.]
Bass Oboe [Oboe basso, Ob.b.]
3 Clarinets in B♭ [Clarinetti, Cl. (B/Si♭)]
Bass Clarinet in B♭ [Clarinetto basso, Cl.b. (B/Si♭)]
3 Bassoons [Fagotti, Fg.]
Sarrusophone* or Contrabassoon
  [Sarrusofono, Sarr., o Contrafagotto]

6 Horns in F [Corni, Cor. (Fa)]
3 Trumpets in C [Trombe, Tr. (Do)]
3 Tenor Trombones [Tromboni, Trb.]
Bass Tuba [Tuba bassa, Tb.b.]

Timpani [Timpani, Timp.]

Percussion
  Tambourine [Tamburino, Tbr.]
  Triangle [Triangolo, Trgl.]
  Cymbals [Piatti, Ptti.]

2 Harps [Arp(e)]

Violins I, II [Violini, Vl.]
Violas [Viole, Vla.]
Cellos [Violoncelli, Vlc.]
Basses [Contrabassi, Cb.]

*a metal double-reed instrument similar to the bassoon in construction;
 traditionally used as a substitute for the contrabassoon in French
 orchestrations

NOTE

The score designation *Grand Orchestra* calls for a string section of
16 players each for Violins I and II; and 12 each for Violas, Cellos
and Basses.

The score designation *Small Orchestra* calls for a string section of
8 players each for Violins I and II; and 6 each for Violas, Cellos
and Basses.

A Dance Rhapsody

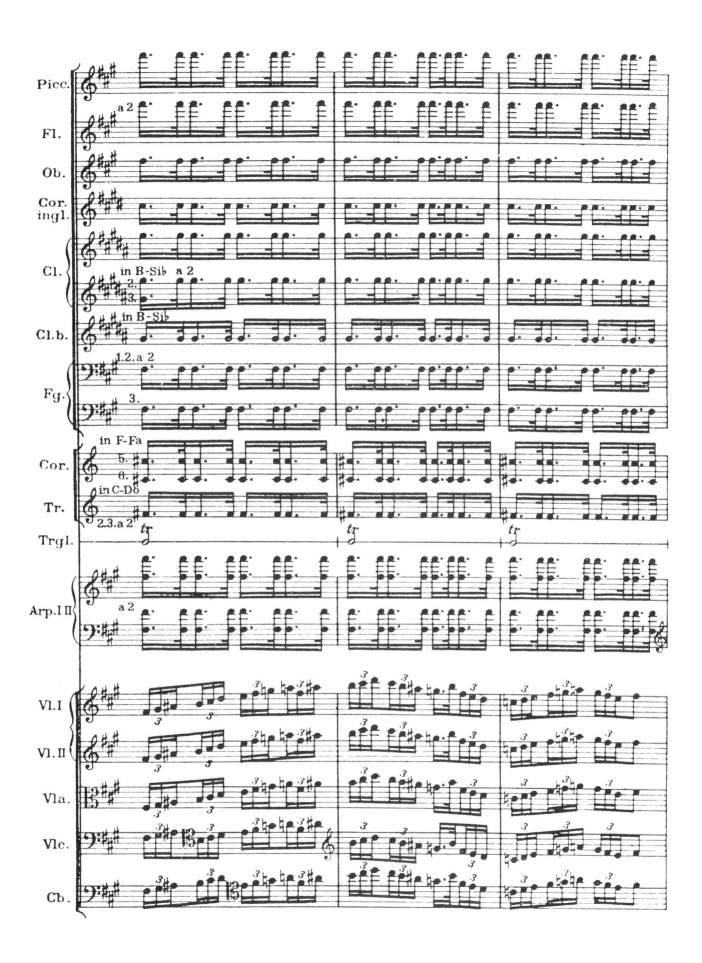

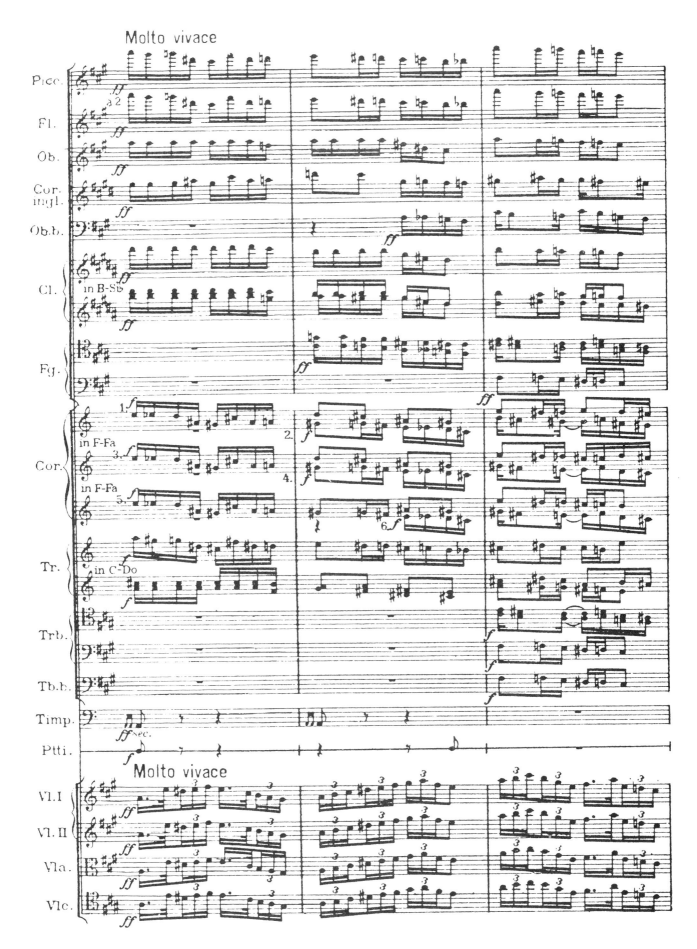

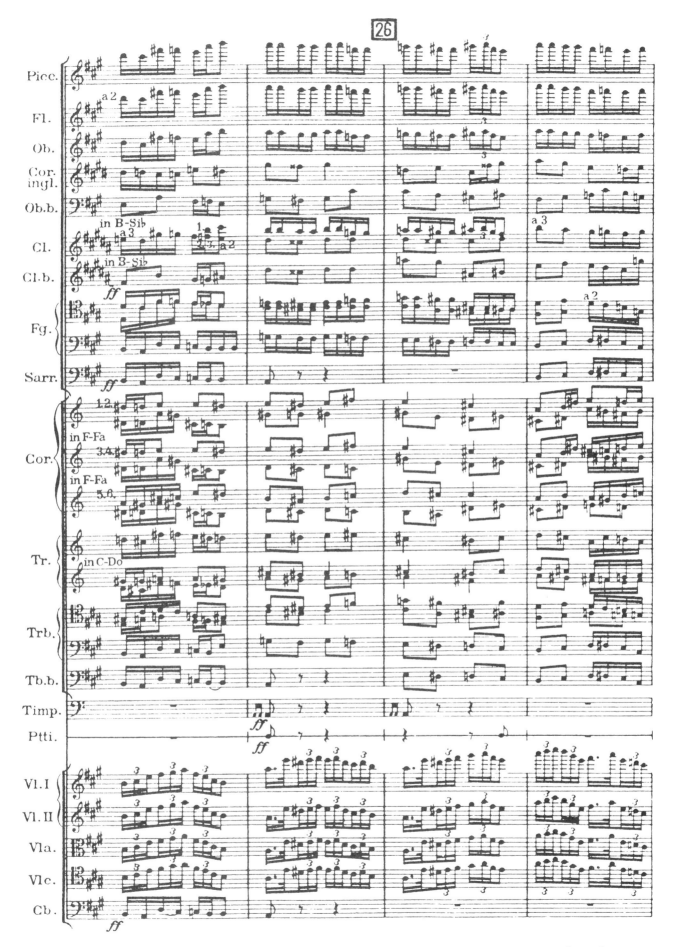

Dedicated to my wife, Jelka Rosen

All are my blooms and all sweet sweet blooms of love
To thee I gave while Spring and Summer Sang

Christina Rosetti

In a Summer Garden

(Spring, 1908)

INSTRUMENTATION

3 Flutes [Fl.]
2 Oboes [Ob.]
English Horn [Eng. Horn]
2 Clarinets in B♭ [Cl.]
Bass Clarinet in B♭ [Bass Cl.]
3 Bassoons [B$^{ns.}$]

4 Horns in F
2 Trumpets in C [Trpts.]
3 Tenor Trombones
Bass Tuba

Timpani [K(ettle) Drums]

Percussion
        Glockenspiel [Glockensp.]
        Triangle

Harp (*or several*)

Violins I, II [V$^{ns.}$]
Violas
Cellos
Basses

In a Summer Garden

In a Summer Garden

Two Pieces
for Small Orchestra

"On Hearing the First Cuckoo in Spring" (1912)
"Summer Night on the River" (1911)

INSTRUMENTATION

2 Flutes [Fls.]
Oboe [Ob.]
2 Clarinets in B♭ [Cl.]
2 Bassoons [B$^{ns.}$]

2 Horns in F [H$^{rs.}$]

Violins I, II [V$^{ns.}$]
Violas
Cellos [Violoncellos]
Basses [Double-basses]

For Balfour Gardiner

"On Hearing the First Cuckoo in Spring"

(Introducing a Norwegian Folk Song)

(1912)

"On Hearing the First Cuckoo in Spring"

"On Hearing the First Cuckoo in Spring"

"Summer Night on the River"

(1911)

138   "Summer Night on the River"

A Song
of the High Hills

(1911)

INSTRUMENTATION

3 Flutes [Fl.]
  Fl. 3 doubles Piccolo [Picc.]
2 Oboes [Ob.]
English Horn [Engl. Hr.]
3 Clarinets in B♭ [Cl.]
Bass Clarinet in B♭ [B^s Cl.]
3 Bassoons [B^{ns}]
Sarrusophone* or Contrabassoon [Sarrus^e]

6 Horns in F [Hrs.]
3 Trumpets in C [Trp^s]
3 Tenor Trombones [Trb.]
Bass Tuba [B^s Tuba]

Timpani [Kettle Drums, K.dr.]
  (*three players*)

Percussion
    Bass Drum [B.dr.]
    Glockenspiel [Glockensp.]
    Cymbals [Cymb.]

Celesta [Cel.]
2 Harps

Chorus**

Violins I, II [Vns]
Violas
Cellos [V(iolon)cellos]
Basses

*See footnote, p. 42.

**The score calls for a wordless 8-part chorus consisting of Sopranos I
& II, Contraltos I & II, Tenors I & II and Basses I & II. Each of the
eight parts requires four voices. Contralto II and Tenors I and II are
briefly subdivided as well. The music also includes passages for Solo
Soprano and Solo Tenor, both marked "in the chorus."

   The original score carries the instruction: "The chorus must be
sung on the vowel which will produce the richest tone possible."

A Song
of the High Hills

A Song of the High Hills

A Song of the High Hills

A Song of the High Hills   END OF EDITION

Dover Orchestral Scores

THE SIX BRANDENBURG CONCERTOS AND THE FOUR ORCHESTRAL SUITES IN FULL SCORE, Johann Sebastian Bach. Complete standard Bach-Gesellschaft editions in large, clear format. Study score. 273pp. 9 × 12. 23376-6 Pa. **$11.95**

COMPLETE CONCERTI FOR SOLO KEYBOARD AND ORCHESTRA IN FULL SCORE, Johann Sebastian Bach. Bach's seven complete concerti for solo keyboard and orchestra in full score from the authoritative Bach-Gesellschaft edition. 206pp. 9 × 12. 24929-8 Pa. **$11.95**

THE THREE VIOLIN CONCERTI IN FULL SCORE, Johann Sebastian Bach. Concerto in A Minor, BWV 1041; Concerto in E Major, BWV 1042; and Concerto for Two Violins in D Minor, BWV 1043. Bach-Gesellschaft edition. 64pp. 9⅜ × 12¼. 25124-1 Pa. **$6.95**

GREAT ORGAN CONCERTI, OPP. 4 & 7, IN FULL SCORE, George Frideric Handel. 12 organ concerti composed by great Baroque master are reproduced in full score from the *Deutsche Handelgesellschaft* edition. 138pp. 9⅜ × 12¼. 24462-8 Pa. **$8.95**

COMPLETE CONCERTI GROSSI IN FULL SCORE, George Frideric Handel. Monumental Opus 6 Concerti Grossi, Opus 3 and "Alexander's Feast" Concerti Grossi—19 in all—reproduced from most authoritative edition. 258pp. 9⅜ × 12¼. 24187-4 Pa. **$13.95**

COMPLETE CONCERTI GROSSI IN FULL SCORE, Arcangelo Corelli. All 12 concerti in the famous late nineteenth-century edition prepared by violinist Joseph Joachim and musicologist Friedrich Chrysander. 240pp. 8⅜ × 11¼. 25606-5 Pa. **$12.95**

WATER MUSIC AND MUSIC FOR THE ROYAL FIREWORKS IN FULL SCORE, George Frideric Handel. Full scores of two of the most popular Baroque orchestral works performed today—reprinted from definitive Deutsche Handelgesellschaft edition. Total of 96pp. 8⅝ × 11. 25070-9 Pa. **$7.95**

LATER SYMPHONIES, Wolfgang A. Mozart. Full orchestral scores to last symphonies (Nos. 35–41) reproduced from definitive Breitkopf & Härtel Complete Works edition. Study score. 285pp. 9 × 12. 23052-X Pa. **$12.95**

17 DIVERTIMENTI FOR VARIOUS INSTRUMENTS, Wolfgang A. Mozart. Sparkling pieces of great vitality and brilliance from 1771–1779; consecutively numbered from 1 to 17. Reproduced from definitive Breitkopf & Härtel Complete Works edition. Study score. 241pp. 9⅜ × 12¼. 23862-8 Pa. **$13.95**

PIANO CONCERTOS NOS. 11-16 IN FULL SCORE, Wolfgang Amadeus Mozart. Authoritative Breitkopf & Härtel edition of six staples of the concerto repertoire, including Mozart's cadenzas for Nos. 12–16. 256pp. 9⅜ × 12¼. 25468-2 Pa. **$12.95**

PIANO CONCERTOS NOS. 17-22, Wolfgang Amadeus Mozart. Six complete piano concertos in full score, with Mozart's own cadenzas for Nos. 17–19. Breitkopf & Härtel edition. Study score. 370pp. 9⅜ × 12¼. 23599-8 Pa. **$16.95**

PIANO CONCERTOS NOS. 23-27, Wolfgang Amadeus Mozart. Mozart's last five piano concertos in full score, plus cadenzas for Nos. 23 and 27, and the Concert Rondo in D Major, K.382. Breitkopf & Härtel edition. Study score. 310pp. 9⅜ × 12¼. 23600-5 Pa. **$13.95**

CONCERTI FOR WIND INSTRUMENTS IN FULL SCORE, Wolfgang Amadeus Mozart. Exceptional volume contains ten pieces for orchestra and wind instruments and includes some of Mozart's finest, most popular music. 272pp. 9⅜ × 12¼. 25228-0 Pa. **$13.95**

THE VIOLIN CONCERTI AND THE SINFONIA CONCERTANTE, K.364, IN FULL SCORE, Wolfgang Amadeus Mozart. All five violin concerti and famed double concerto reproduced from authoritative Breitkopf & Härtel Complete Works Edition. 208pp. 9⅜ × 12½. 25169-1 Pa. **$12.95**

SYMPHONIES 88-92 IN FULL SCORE: The Haydn Society Edition, Joseph Haydn. Full score of symphonies Nos. 88 through 92. Large, readable noteheads, ample margins for fingerings, etc., and extensive Editor's Commentary. 304pp. 9 × 12. (Available in U.S. only) 24445-8 Pa. **$15.95**

THE MAGIC FLUTE (DIE ZAUBERFLÖTE) IN FULL SCORE, Wolfgang Amadeus Mozart. Authoritative C. F. Peters edition of Mozart's last opera featuring all the spoken dialogue. Translation of German frontmatter. Dramatis personae. List of Numbers. 226pp. 9 × 12. 24783-X Pa. **$12.95**

FOUR SYMPHONIES IN FULL SCORE, Franz Schubert. Schubert's four most popular symphonies: No. 4 in C Minor ("Tragic"); No. 5 in B-flat Major; No. 8 in B Minor ("Unfinished"); and No. 9 in C Major ("Great"). Breitkopf & Härtel edition. Study score. 261pp. 9⅜ × 12¼. 23681-1 Pa. **$13.95**

GREAT OVERTURES IN FULL SCORE, Carl Maria von Weber. Overtures to *Oberon, Der Freischutz, Euryanthe* and *Preciosa* reprinted from auhoritative Breitkopf & Härtel editions. 112pp. 9 × 12. 25225-6 Pa. **$9.95**

SYMPHONIES NOS. 1, 2, 3, AND 4 IN FULL SCORE, Ludwig van Beethoven. Republication of H. Litolff edition. 272pp. 9 × 12. 26033-X Pa. **$11.95**

SYMPHONIES NOS. 5, 6 AND 7 IN FULL SCORE, Ludwig van Beethoven. Republication of the H. Litolff edition. 272pp. 9 × 12. 26034-8 Pa. **$11.95**

SYMPHONIES NOS. 8 AND 9 IN FULL SCORE, Ludwig van Beethoven. Republication of the H. Litolff edition. 256pp. 9 × 12. 26035-6 Pa. **$11.95**

SIX GREAT OVERTURES IN FULL SCORE, Ludwig van Beethoven. Six staples of the orchestral repertoire from authoritative Breitkopf & Härtel edition. *Leonore Overtures,* Nos. 1–3; Overtures to *Coriolanus, Egmont, Fidelio.* 288pp. 9 × 12. 24789-9 Pa. **$13.95**

COMPLETE PIANO CONCERTOS IN FULL SCORE, Ludwig van Beethoven. Complete scores of five great Beethoven piano concertos, with all cadenzas as he wrote them, reproduced from authoritative Breitkopf & Härtel edition. New table of contents. 384pp. 9⅜ × 12¼. 24563-2 Pa. **$15.95**

GREAT ROMANTIC VIOLIN CONCERTI IN FULL SCORE, Ludwig van Beethoven, Felix Mendelssohn and Peter Ilyitch Tchaikovsky. The Beethoven Op. 61, Mendelssohn, Op. 64 and Tchaikovsky, Op. 35 concertos reprinted from the Breitkopf & Härtel editions. 224pp. 9 × 12. 24989-1 Pa. **$10.95**

MAJOR ORCHESTRAL WORKS IN FULL SCORE, Felix Mendelssohn. Generally considered to be Mendelssohn's finest orchestral works, here in one volume are: the complete *Midsummer Night's Dream; Hebrides Overture; Calm Sea and Prosperous Voyage Overture;* Symphony No. 3 in A ("Scottish"); and Symphony No. 4 in A ("Italian"). Breitkopf & Härtel edition. Study score. 406pp. 9 × 12. 23184-4 Pa. **$18.95**

COMPLETE SYMPHONIES, Johannes Brahms. Full orchestral scores. No. 1 in C Minor, Op. 68; No. 2 in D Major, Op. 73; No. 3 in F Major, Op. 90; and No. 4 in E Minor, Op. 98. Reproduced from definitive Vienna Gesellschaft der Musikfreunde edition. Study score. 344pp. 9 × 12. 23053-8 Pa. **$14.95**

*Available from your music dealer or write for **free** Music Catalog to Dover Publications, Inc., Dept. MUBI, 31 East 2nd Street, Mineola, N.Y. 11501.*

Dover Orchestral Scores

THREE ORCHESTRAL WORKS IN FULL SCORE: Academic Festival Overture, Tragic Overture and Variations on a Theme by Joseph Haydn, Johannes Brahms. Reproduced from the authoritative Breitkopf & Härtel edition three of Brahms's great orchestral favorites. Editor's commentary in German and English. 112pp. 9⅜ × 12¼.
24637-X Pa. **$8.95**

COMPLETE CONCERTI IN FULL SCORE, Johannes Brahms. Piano Concertos Nos. 1 and 2; Violin Concerto, Op. 77; Concerto for Violin and Cello, Op. 102. Definitive Breitkopf & Härtel edition. 352pp. 9⅜ × 12¼.
24170-X Pa. **$15.95**

COMPLETE SYMPHONIES IN FULL SCORE, Robert Schumann. No. 1 in B-flat Major, Op. 38 ("Spring"); No. 2 in C Major, Op. 61; No. 3 in E Flat Major, Op. 97 ("Rhenish"); and No. 4 in D Minor, Op. 120. Breitkopf & Härtel editions. Study score. 416pp. 9⅜ × 12¼.
24013-4 Pa. **$18.95**

GREAT WORKS FOR PIANO AND ORCHESTRA IN FULL SCORE, Robert Schumann. Collection of three superb pieces for piano and orchestra, including the popular Piano Concerto in A Minor. Breitkopf & Härtel edition. 183pp. 9⅜ × 12¼.   24340-0 Pa. **$10.95**

THE PIANO CONCERTOS IN FULL SCORE, Frédéric Chopin. The authoritative Breitkopf & Härtel full-score edition in one volume of Piano Concertos No. 1 in E Minor and No. 2 in F Minor. 176pp. 9 × 12.
25835-1 Pa. **$10.95**

THE PIANO CONCERTI IN FULL SCORE, Franz Liszt. Available in one volume the Piano Concerto No. 1 in E-flat Major and the Piano Concerto No. 2 in A Major—are among the most studied, recorded and performed of all works for piano and orchestra. 144pp. 9 × 12.
25221-3 Pa. **$8.95**

SYMPHONY NO. 8 IN G MAJOR, OP. 88, SYMPHONY NO. 9 IN E MINOR, OP. 95 ("NEW WORLD") IN FULL SCORE, Antonín Dvořák. Two celebrated symphonies by the great Czech composer, the Eighth and the immensely popular Ninth, "From the New World" in one volume. 272pp. 9 × 12.   24749-X Pa. **$13.95**

FOUR ORCHESTRAL WORKS IN FULL SCORE: Rapsodie Espagnole, Mother Goose Suite, Valses Nobles et Sentimentales, and Pavane for a Dead Princess, Maurice Ravel. Four of Ravel's most popular orchestral works, reprinted from original full-score French editions. 240pp. 9⅜ × 12¼. (Not available in France or Germany)
25962-5 Pa. **$12.95**

DAPHNIS AND CHLOE IN FULL SCORE, Maurice Ravel. Definitive full-score edition of Ravel's rich musical setting of a Greek fable by Longus is reprinted here from the original French edition. 320pp. 9⅜ × 12¼. (Not available in France or Germany)   25826-2 Pa. **$15.95**

THREE GREAT ORCHESTRAL WORKS IN FULL SCORE, Claude Debussy. Three favorites by influential modernist: Prélude à l'Après-midi d'un Faune, Nocturnes, and La Mer. Reprinted from early French editions. 279pp. 9 × 12.   24441-5 Pa. **$13.95**

SYMPHONY IN D MINOR IN FULL SCORE, César Franck. Superb, authoritative edition of Franck's only symphony, an often-performed and recorded masterwork of late French romantic style. 160pp. 9 × 12.
25373-2 Pa. **$9.95**

THE GREAT WALTZES IN FULL SCORE, Johann Strauss, Jr. Complete scores of eight melodic masterpieces: The Beautiful Blue Danube, Emperor Waltz, Tales of the Vienna Woods, Wiener Blut, four more. Authoritative editions. 336pp. 8⅜ × 11¼.   26009-7 Pa. **$14.95**

FOURTH, FIFTH AND SIXTH SYMPHONIES IN FULL SCORE, Peter Ilyitch Tchaikovsky. Complete orchestral scores of Symphony No. 4 in F minor, Op. 36; Symphony No. 5 in E minor, Op. 64; Symphony No. 6 in B minor, "Pathetique," Op. 74. Study score. Breitkopf & Härtel editions. 480pp. 9⅜ × 12¼.   23861-X Pa. **$19.95**

ROMEO AND JULIET OVERTURE AND CAPRICCIO ITALIEN IN FULL SCORE, Peter Ilyitch Tchaikovsky. Two of Russian master's most popular compositions in high quality, inexpensive reproduction. From authoritative Russian edition. 208pp. 8⅜ × 11½.
25217-5 Pa. **$10.95**

NUTCRACKER SUITE IN FULL SCORE, Peter Ilyitch Tchaikovsky. Among the most popular ballet pieces ever created—a complete, inexpensive, high-quality score to study and enjoy. 128pp. 9 × 12.
25379-1 Pa. **$8.95**

TONE POEMS, SERIES I: DON JUAN, TOD UND VERKLARUNG, and DON QUIXOTE, Richard Strauss. Three of the most often performed and recorded works in entire orchestral repertoire, reproduced in full score from original editions. Study score. 286pp. 9⅜ × 12¼. (Available in U.S. only)   23754-0 Pa. **$13.95**

TONE POEMS, SERIES II: TILL EULENSPIEGELS LUSTIGE STREICHE, ALSO SPRACH ZARATHUSTRA, and EIN HELDENLEBEN, Richard Strauss. Three important orchestral works, including very popular Till Eulenspiegel's Merry Pranks, reproduced in full score from original editions. Study score. 315pp. 9⅜ × 12¼. (Available in U.S. only)   23755-9 Pa. **$14.95**

DAS LIED VON DER ERDE IN FULL SCORE, Gustav Mahler. Mahler's masterpiece, a fusion of song and symphony, reprinted from the original 1912 Universal Edition. English translations of song texts. 160pp. 9 × 12.   25657-X Pa. **$9.95**

SYMPHONIES NOS. 1 AND 2 IN FULL SCORE, Gustav Mahler. Unabridged, authoritative Austrian editions of Symphony No. 1 in D Major ("Titan") and Symphony No. 2 in C Minor ("Resurrection"). 384pp. 8⅛ × 11.   25473-9 Pa. **$14.95**

SYMPHONIES NOS. 3 AND 4 IN FULL SCORE, Gustav Mahler. Two brilliantly contrasting masterworks—one scored for a massive ensemble, the other for small orchestra and soloist—reprinted from authoritative Viennese editions. 368pp. 9⅜ × 12¼.   26166-2 Pa. **$16.95**

SYMPHONY NO. 8 IN FULL SCORE, Gustav Mahler. Superb authoritative edition of massive, complex "Symphony of a Thousand." Scored for orchestra, eight solo voices, double chorus, boys' choir and organ. Reprint of Izdatel'stvo "Muzyka," Moscow, edition. Translation of texts. 272pp. 9⅜ × 12¼.   26022-4 Pa. **$12.95**

THE FIREBIRD IN FULL SCORE (Original 1910 Version), Igor Stravinsky. Handsome, inexpensive edition of modern masterpiece, renowned for brilliant orchestration, glowing color. Authoritative Russian edition. 176pp. 9⅜ × 12¼. (Available in U.S. only)
25535-2 Pa. **$10.95**

PETRUSHKA IN FULL SCORE: Original Version, Igor Stravinsky. The definitive full-score edition of Stravinsky's masterful score for the great Ballets Russes 1911 production of Petrushka. 160pp. 9⅜ × 12¼. (Available in U.S. only)   25680-4 Pa. **$9.95**

THE RITE OF SPRING IN FULL SCORE, Igor Stravinsky. A reprint of the original full-score edition of the most famous musical work of the 20th century, created as a ballet score for Diaghilev's Ballets Russes. 176pp. 9⅜ × 12¼. (Available in U.S. only)   25857-2 Pa. **$9.95**